Easter Bunny

Coloring Book

By

S.B. Nozaz

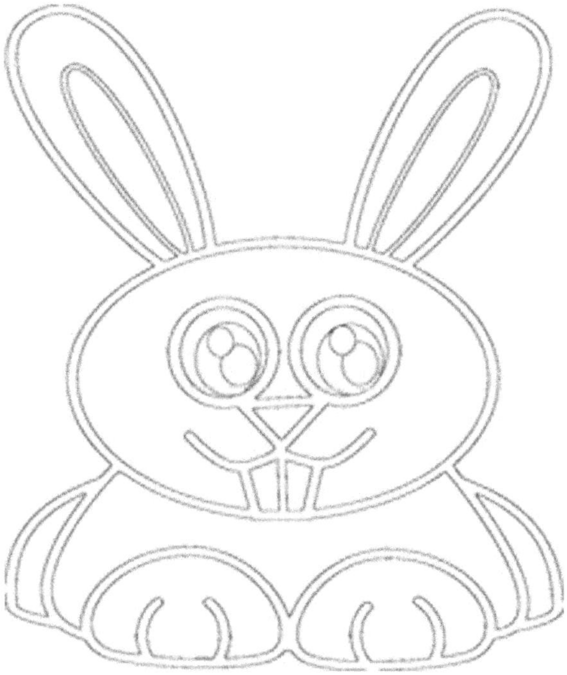

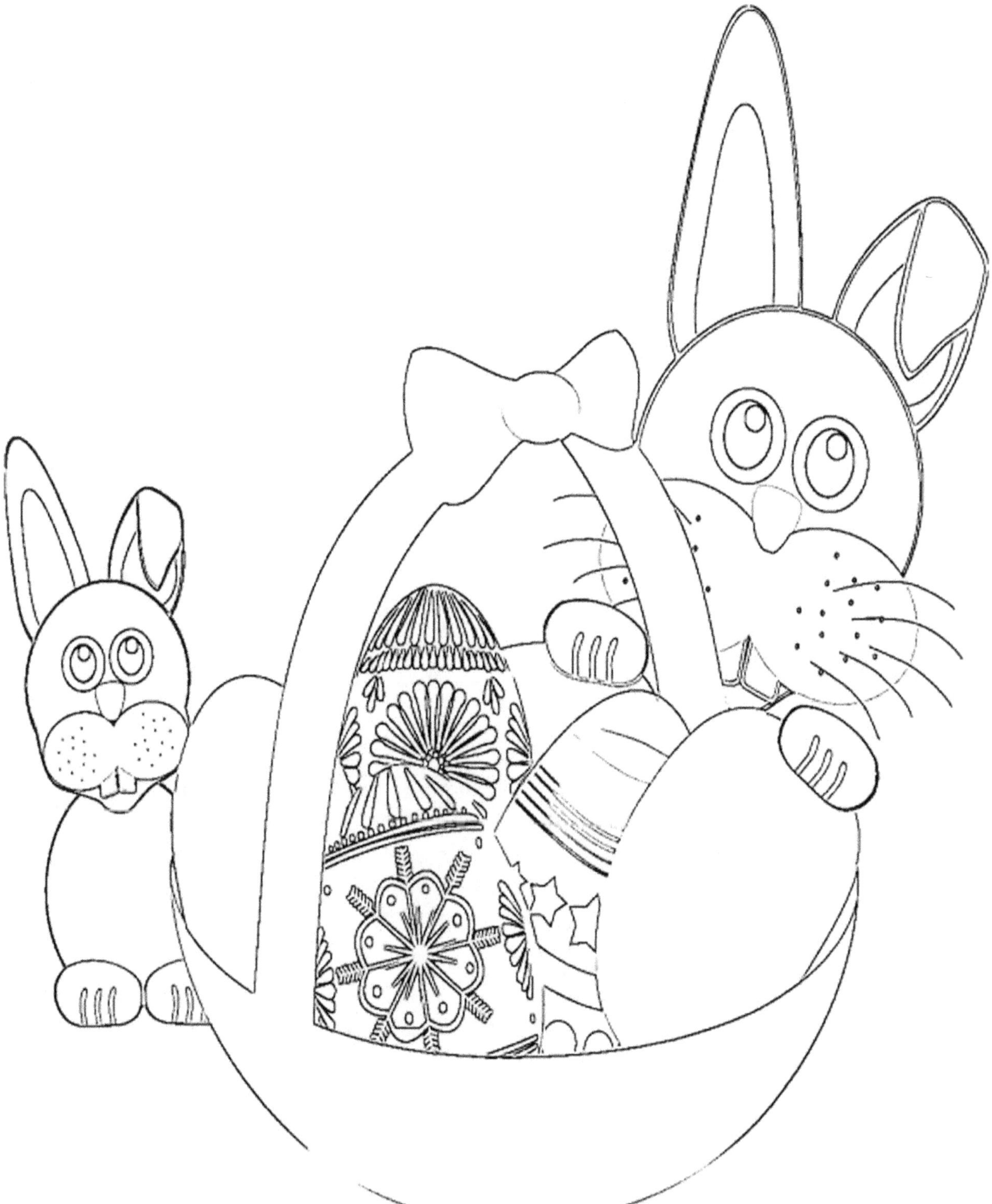

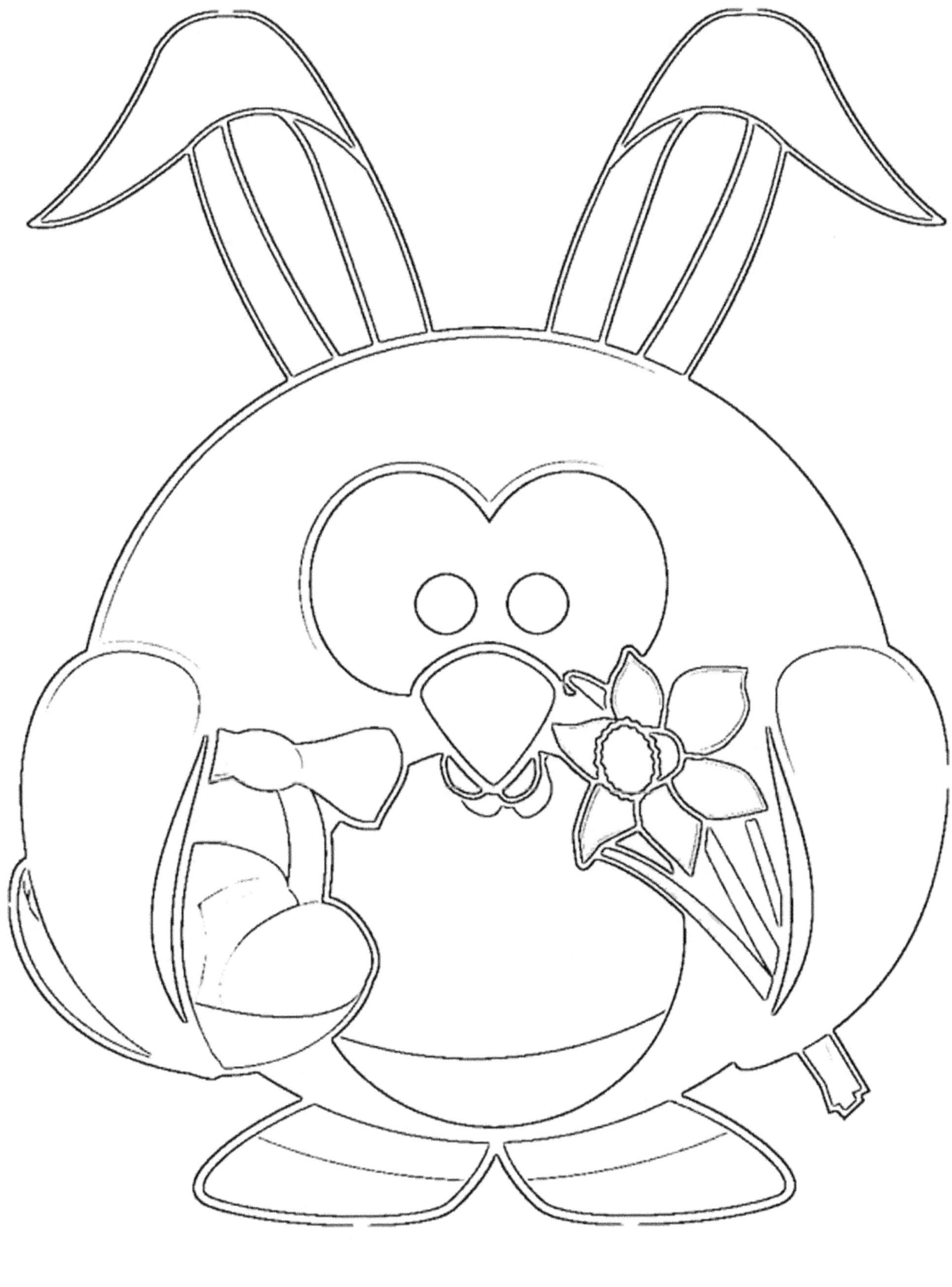

SPRING

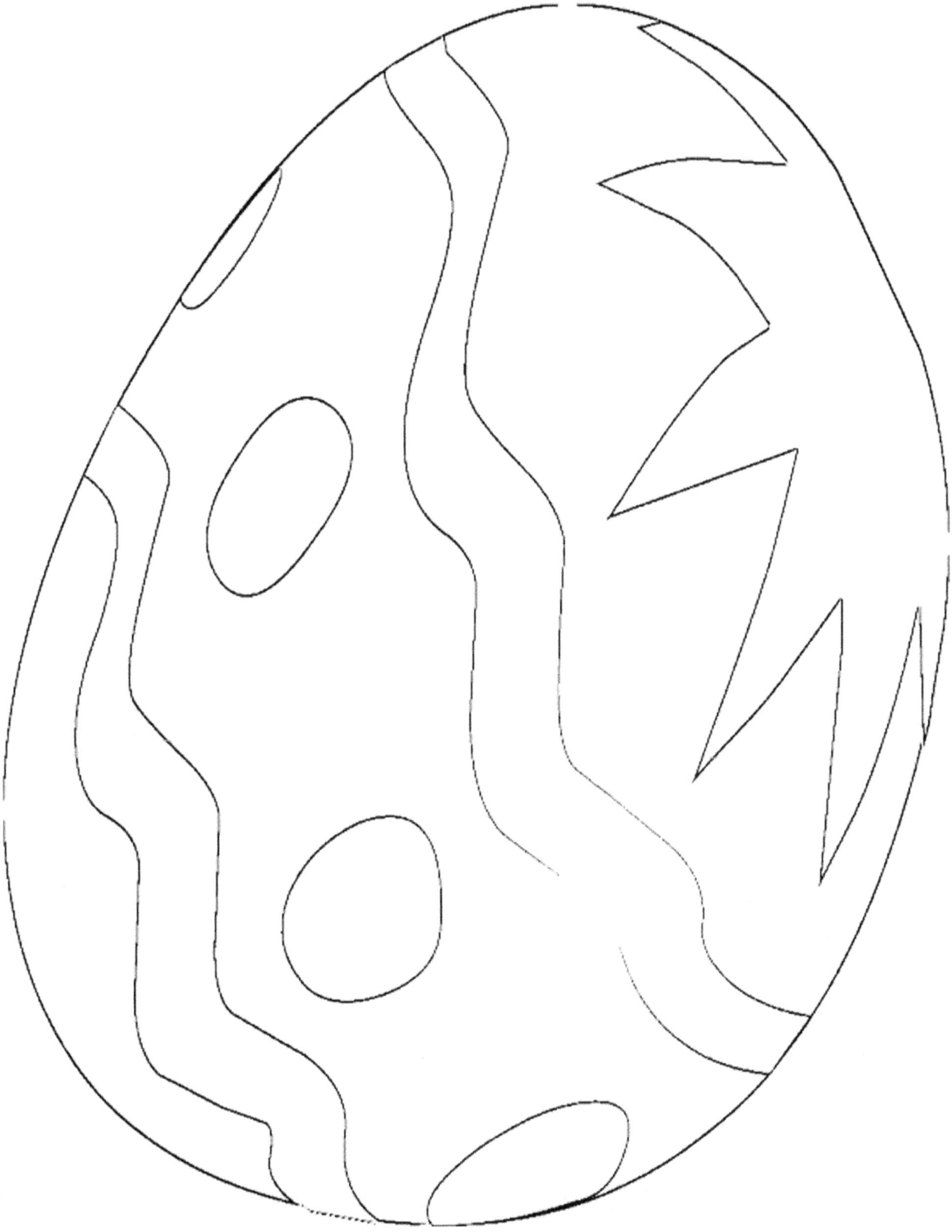

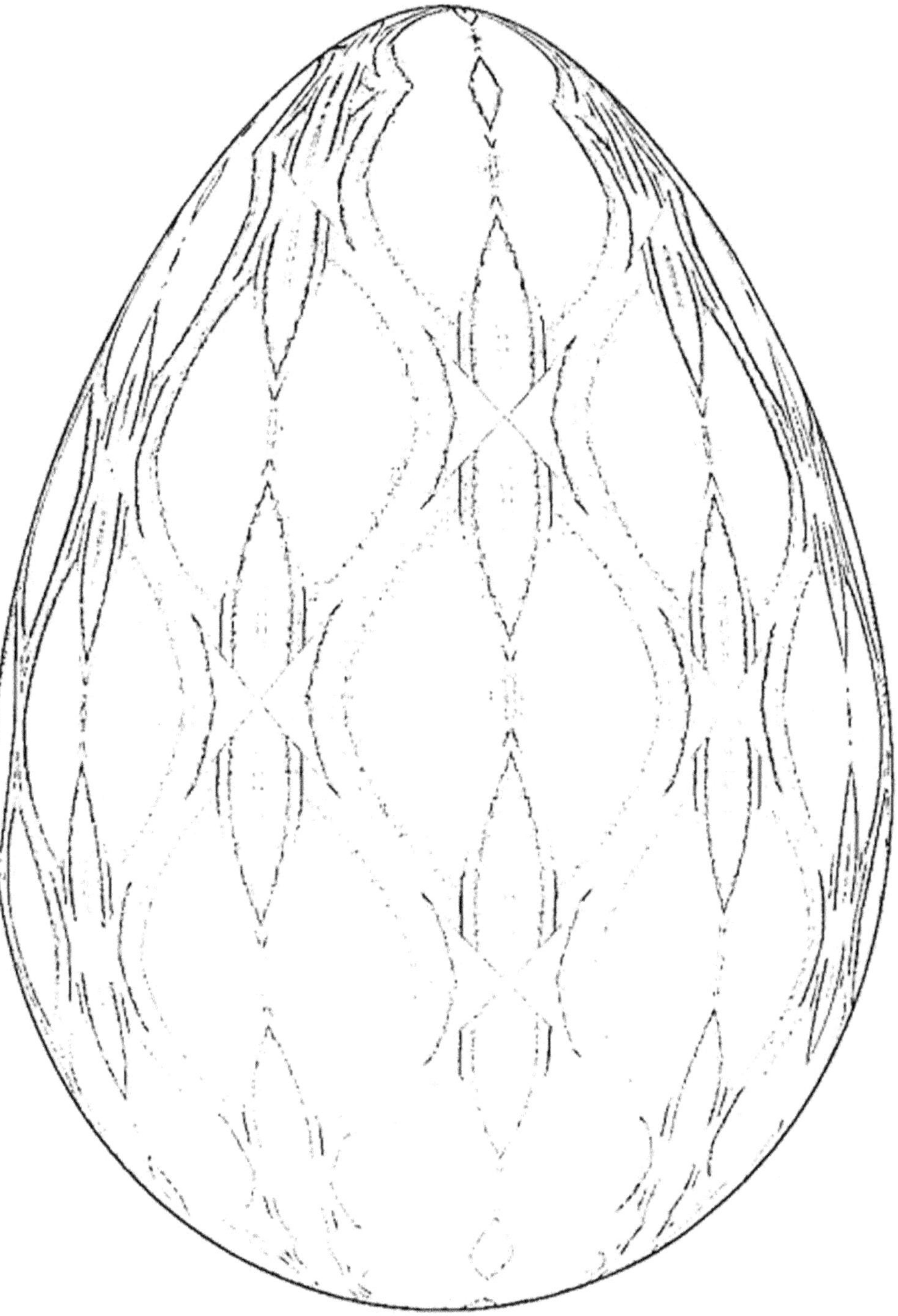

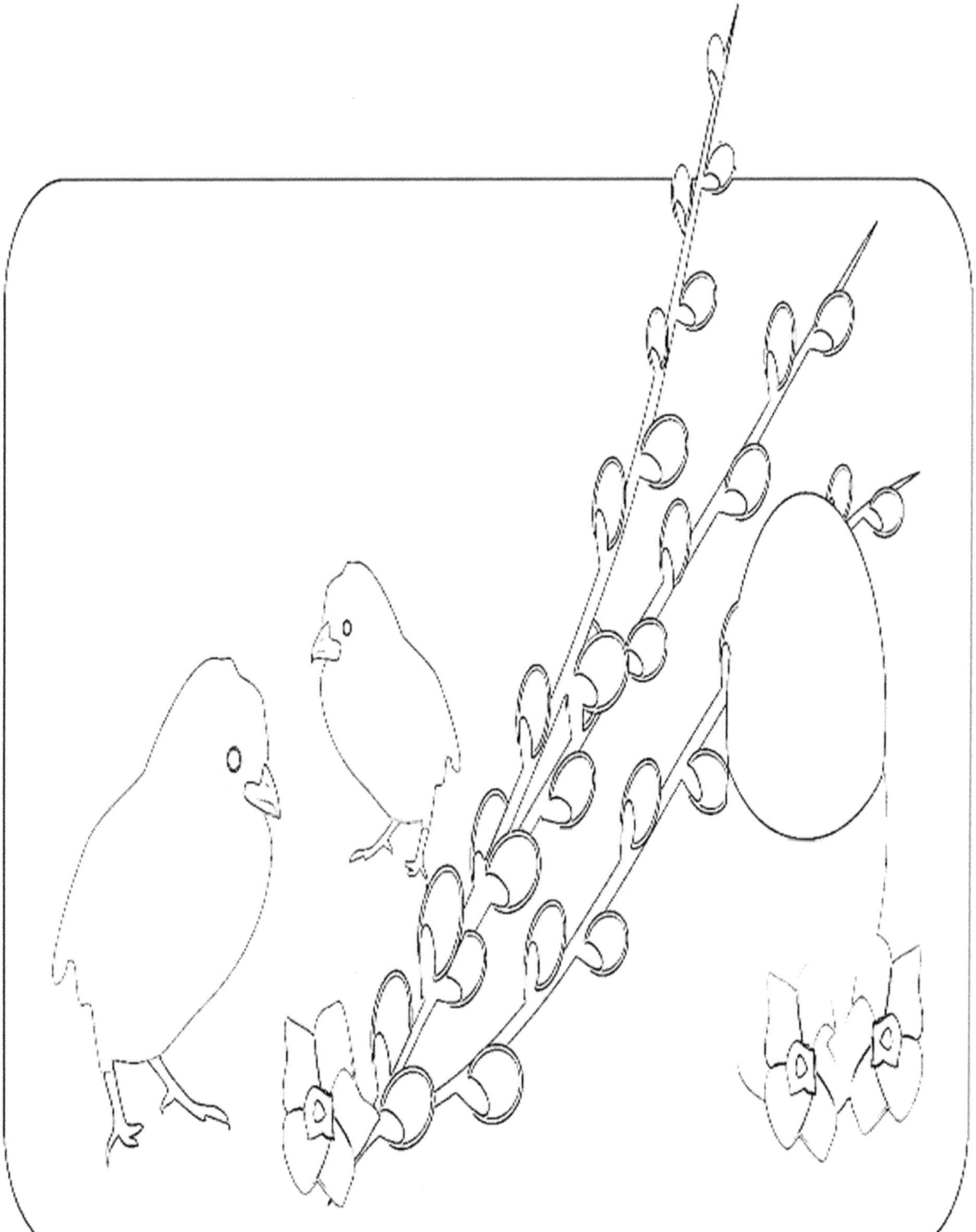

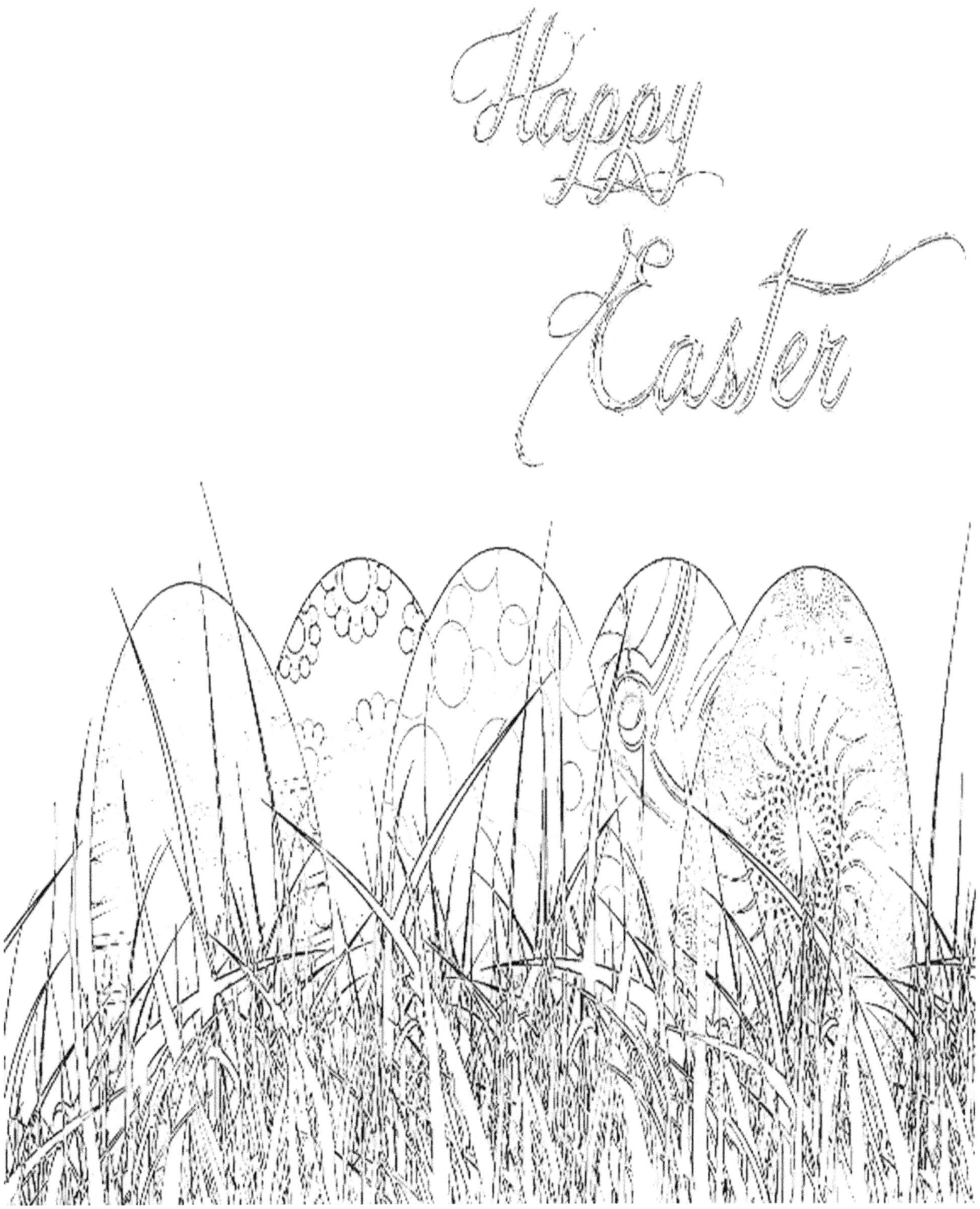
Happy
Easter

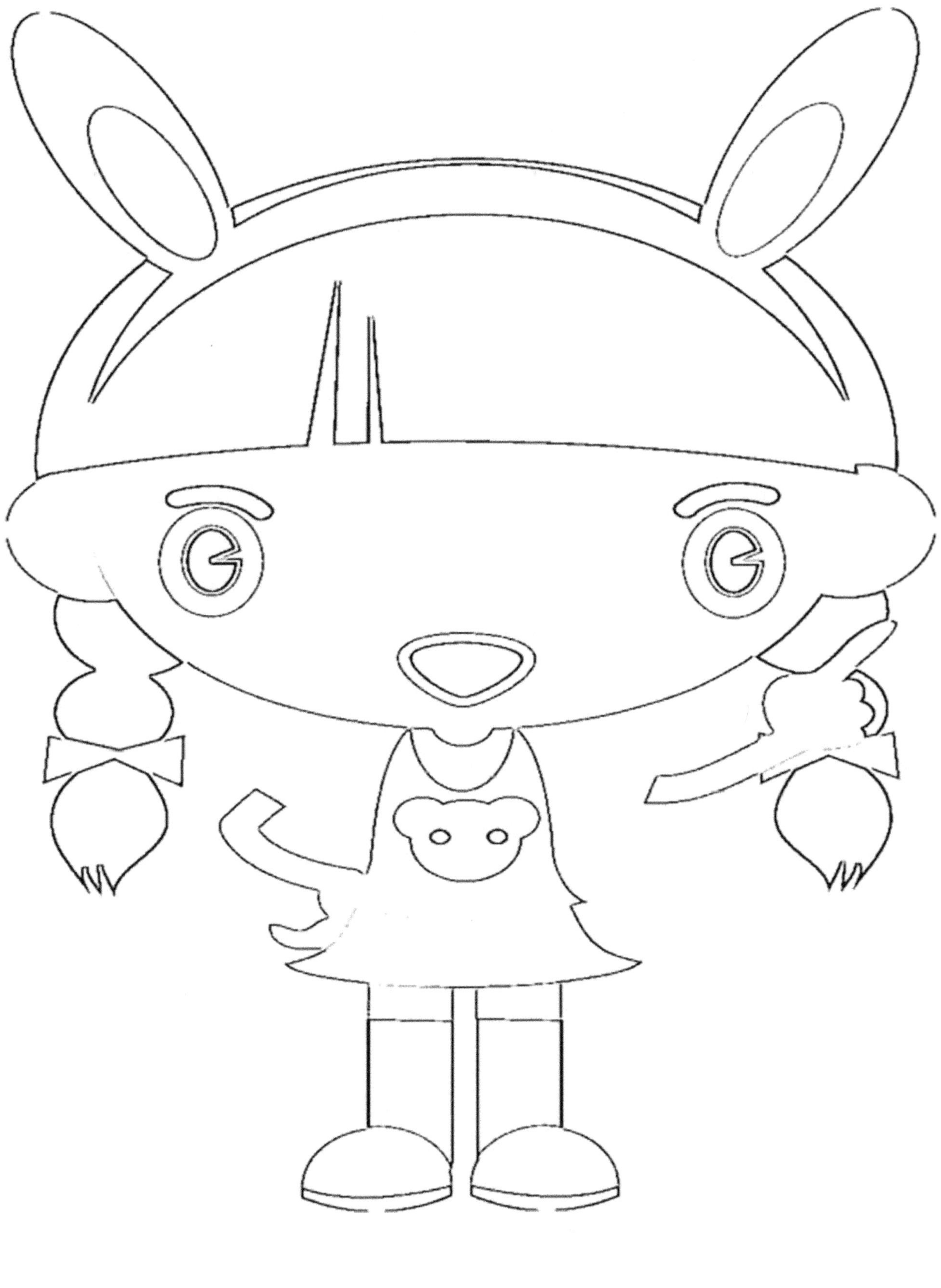

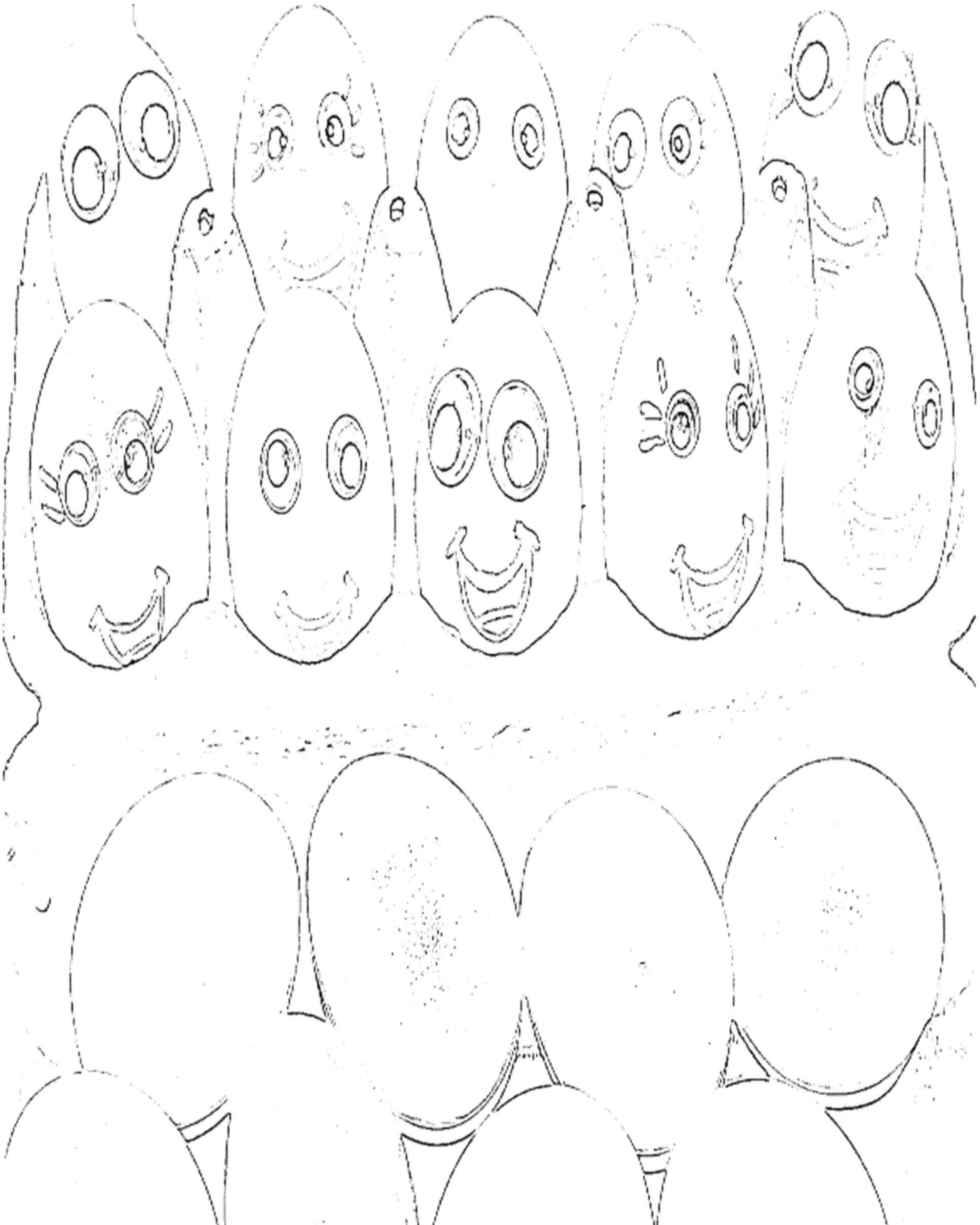

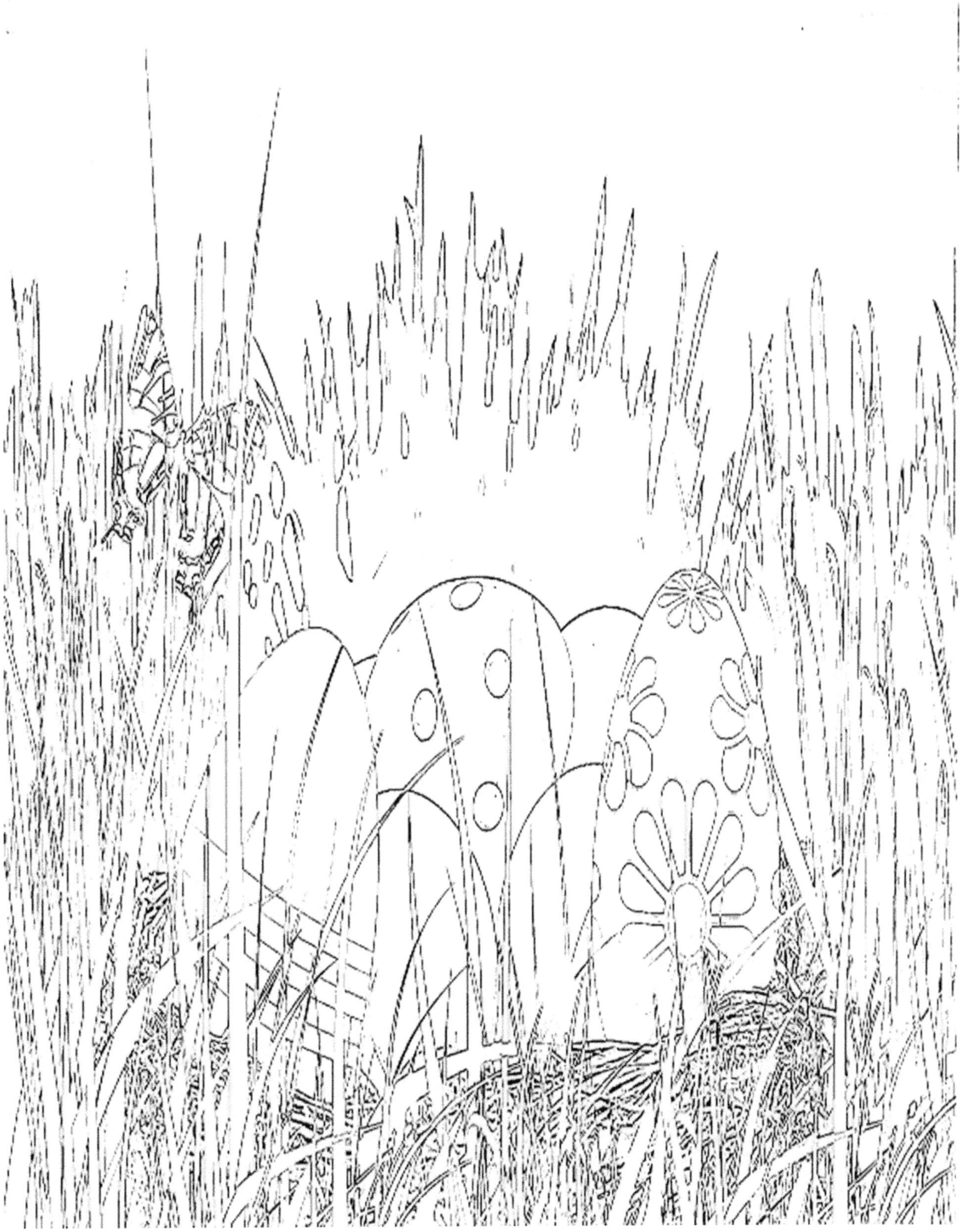

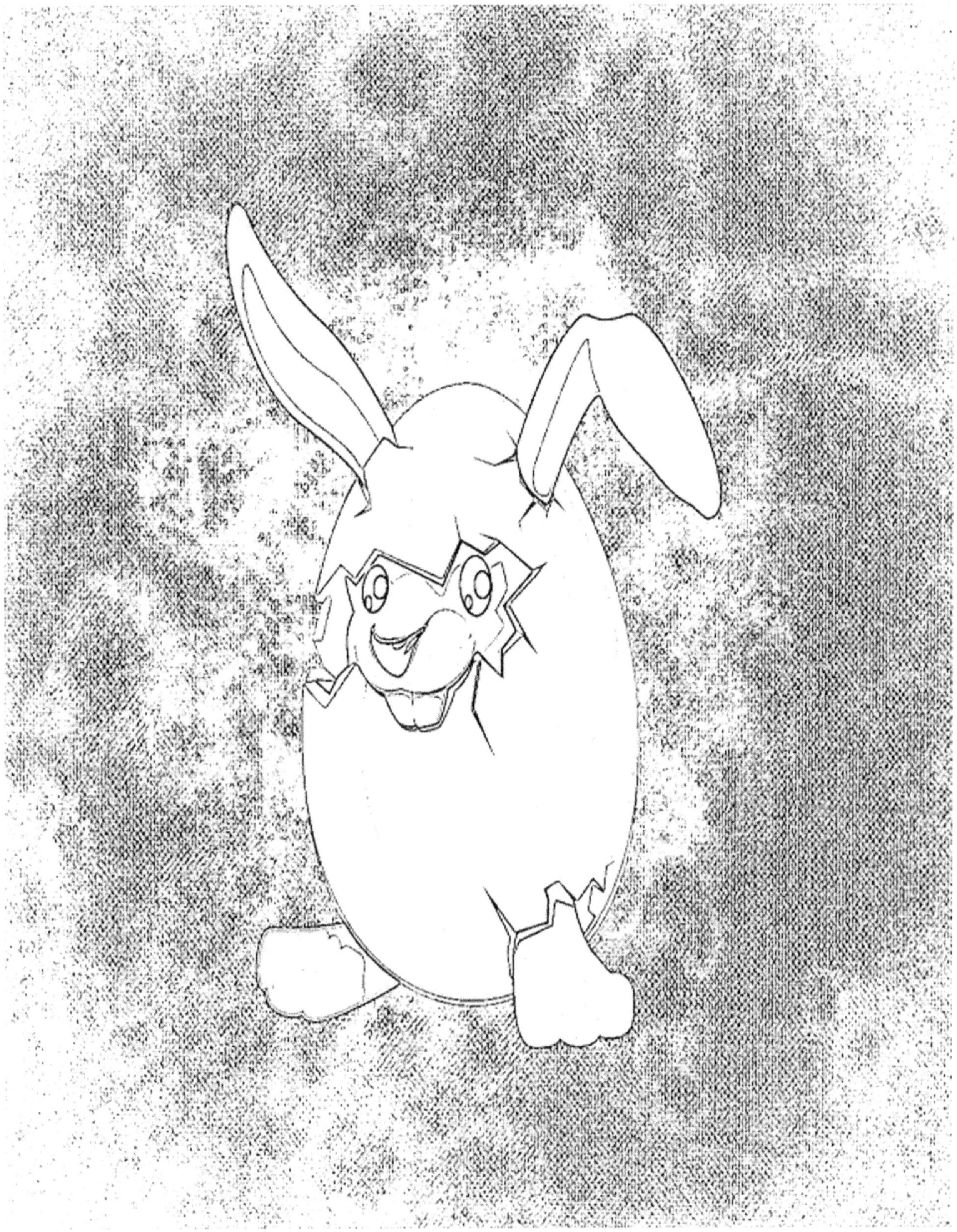

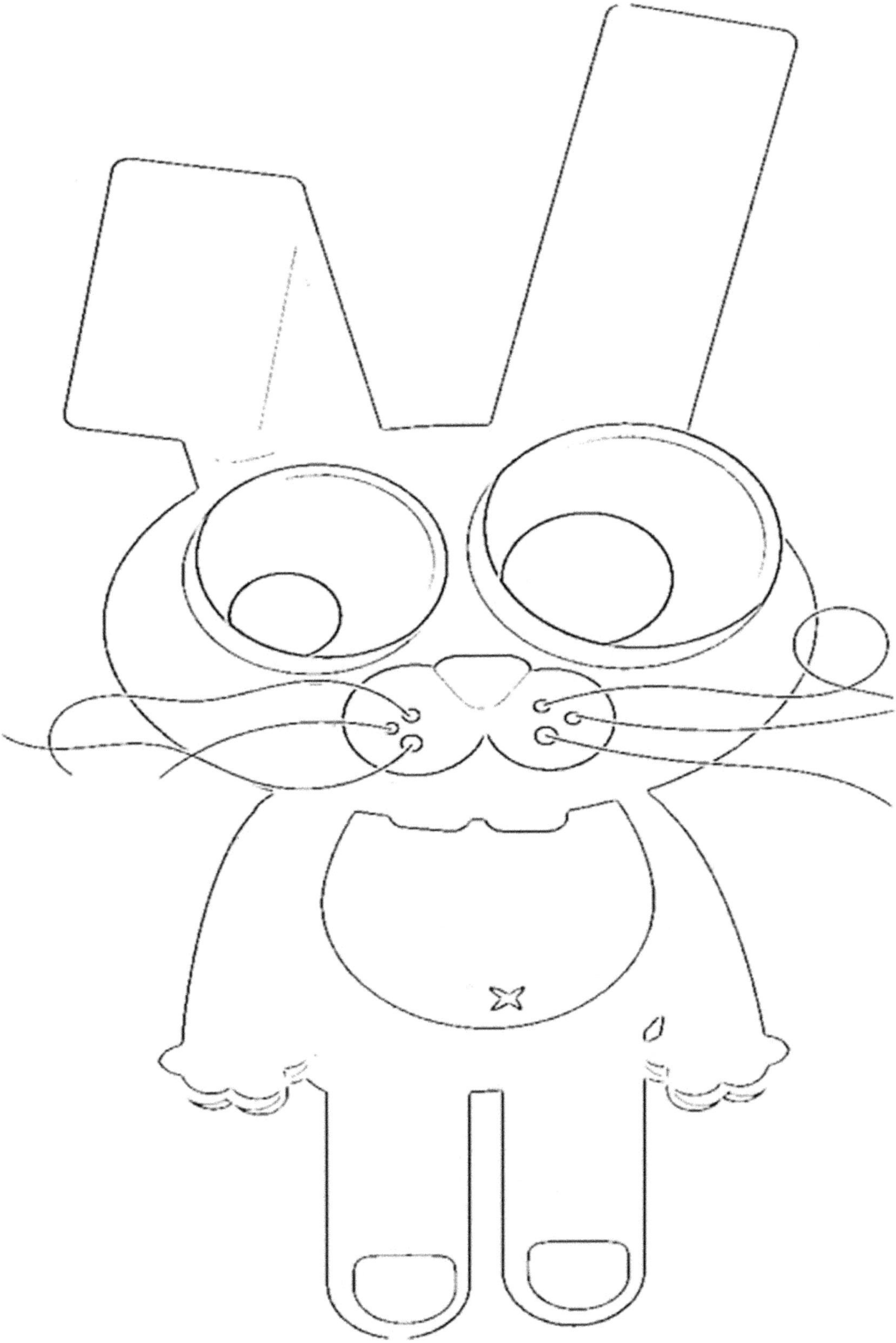

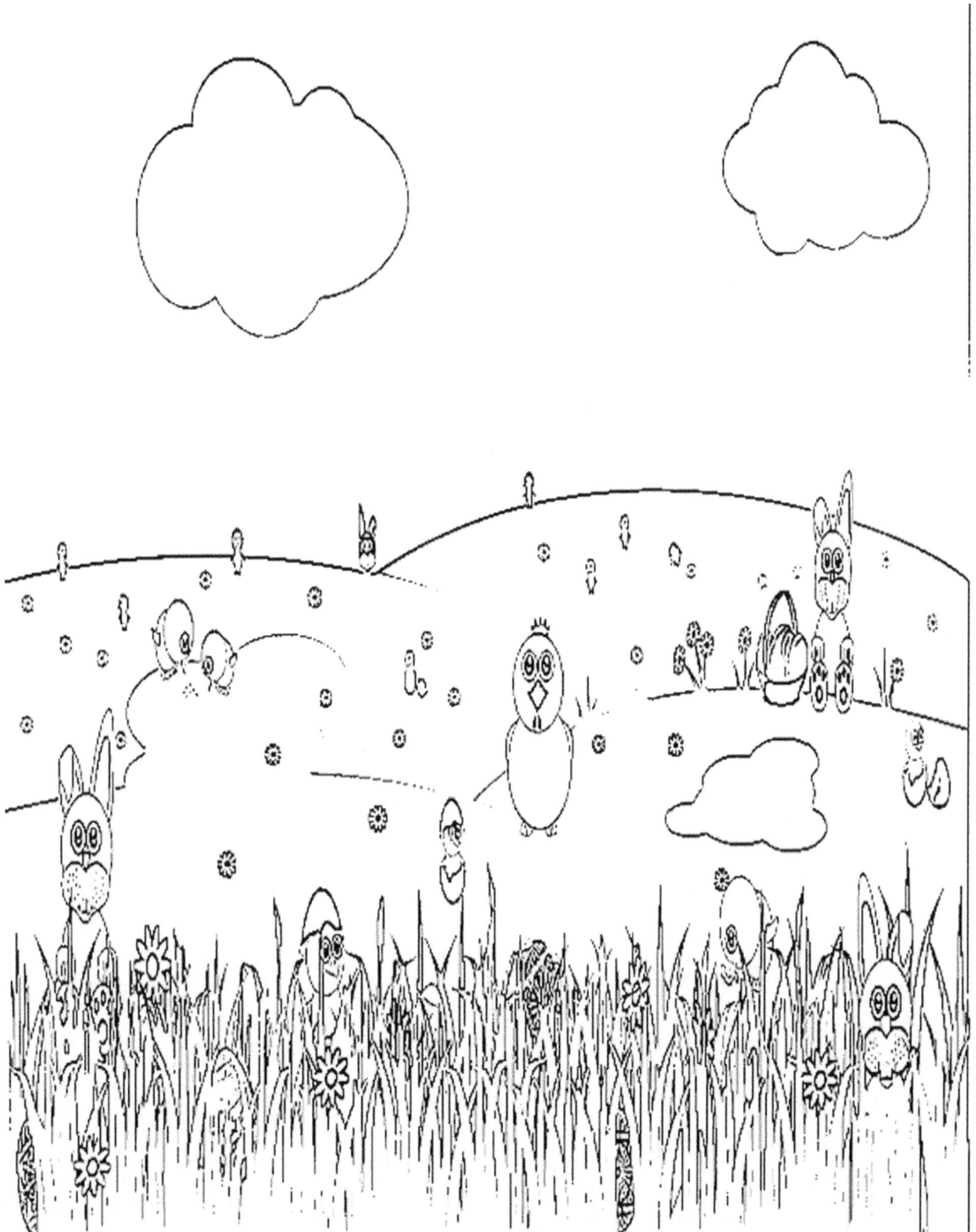

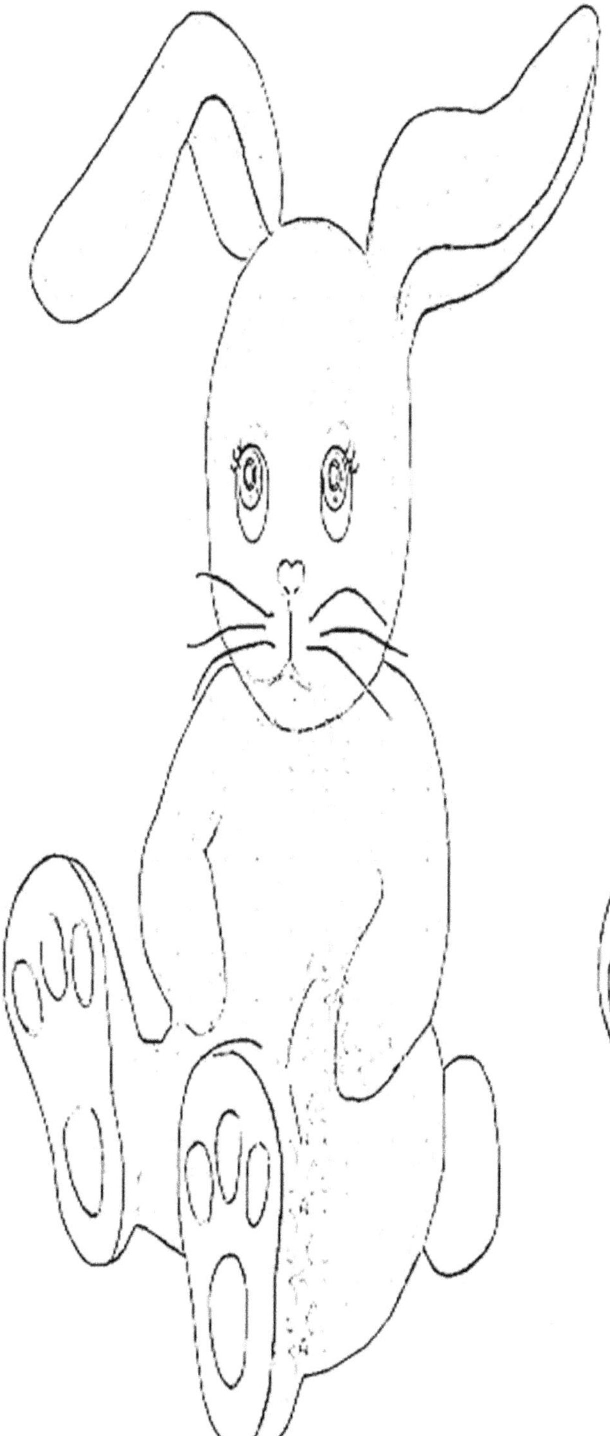
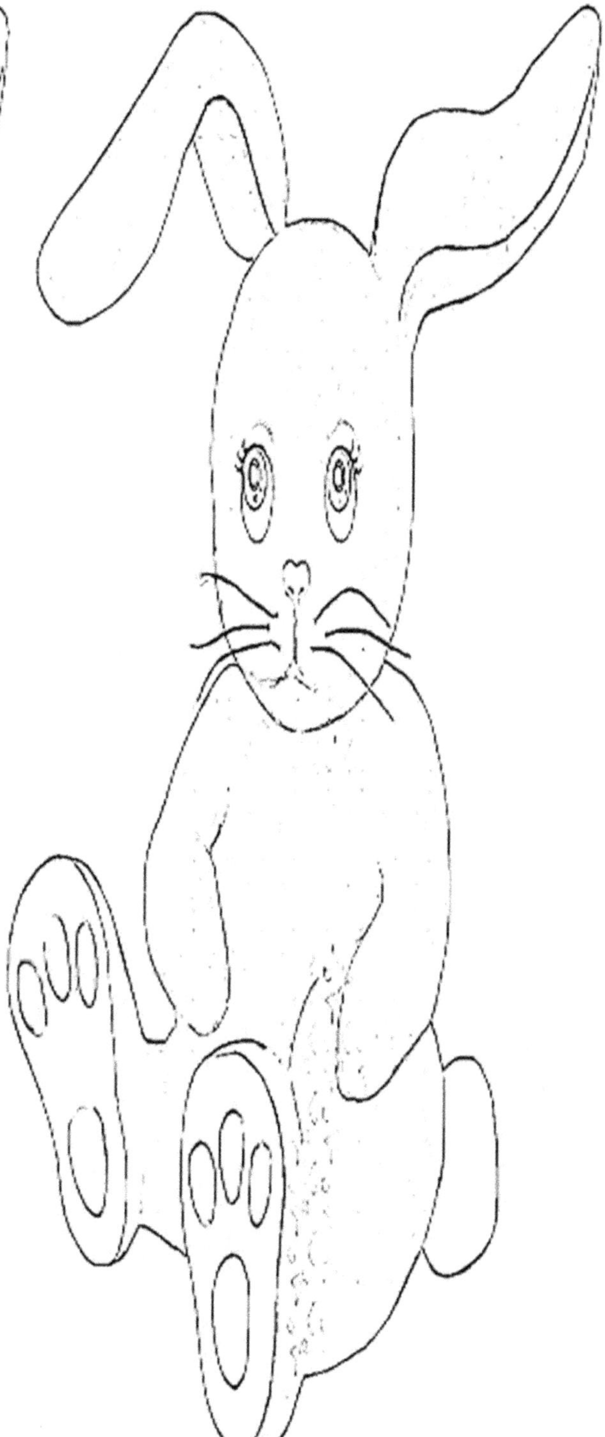

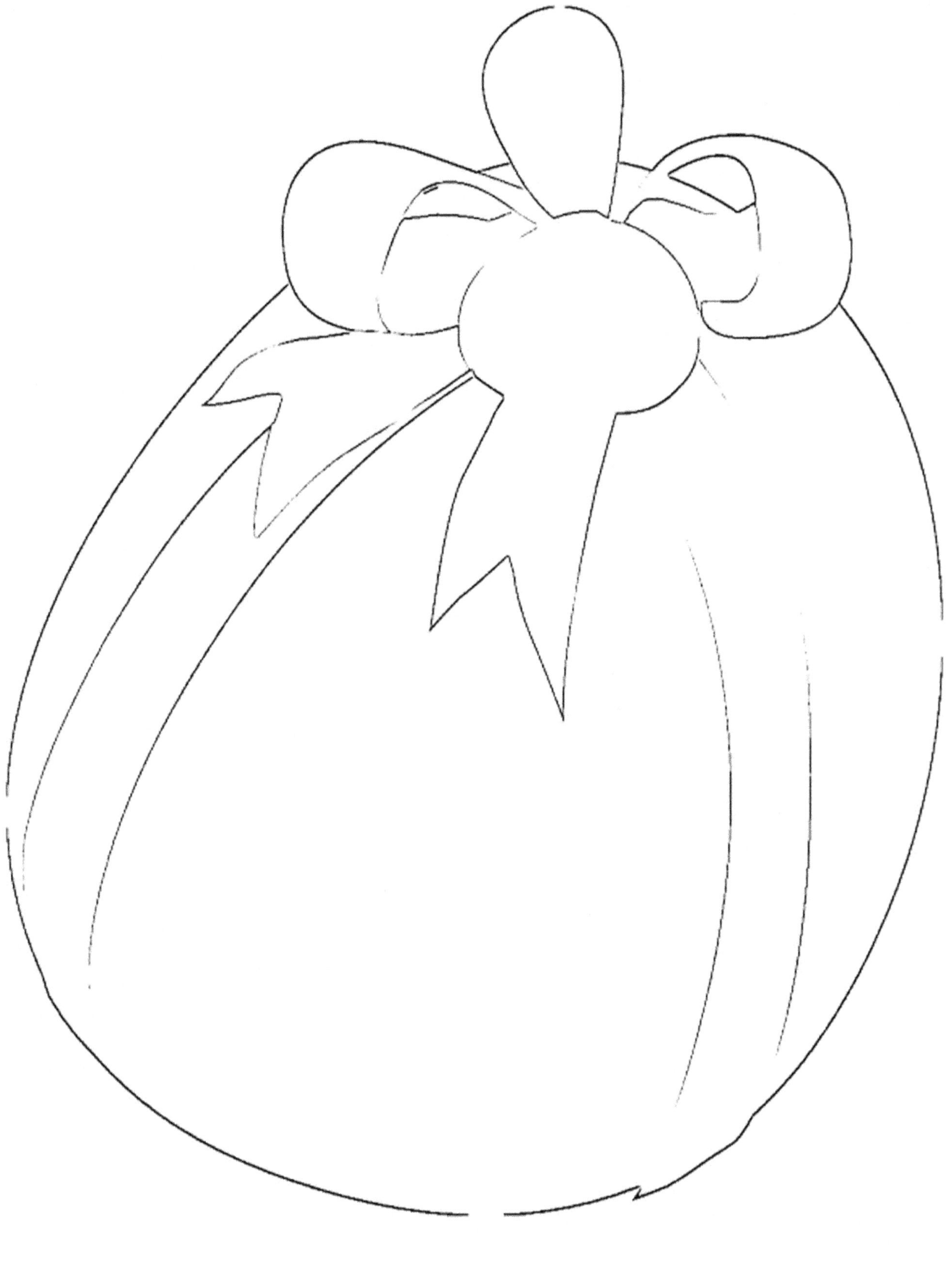

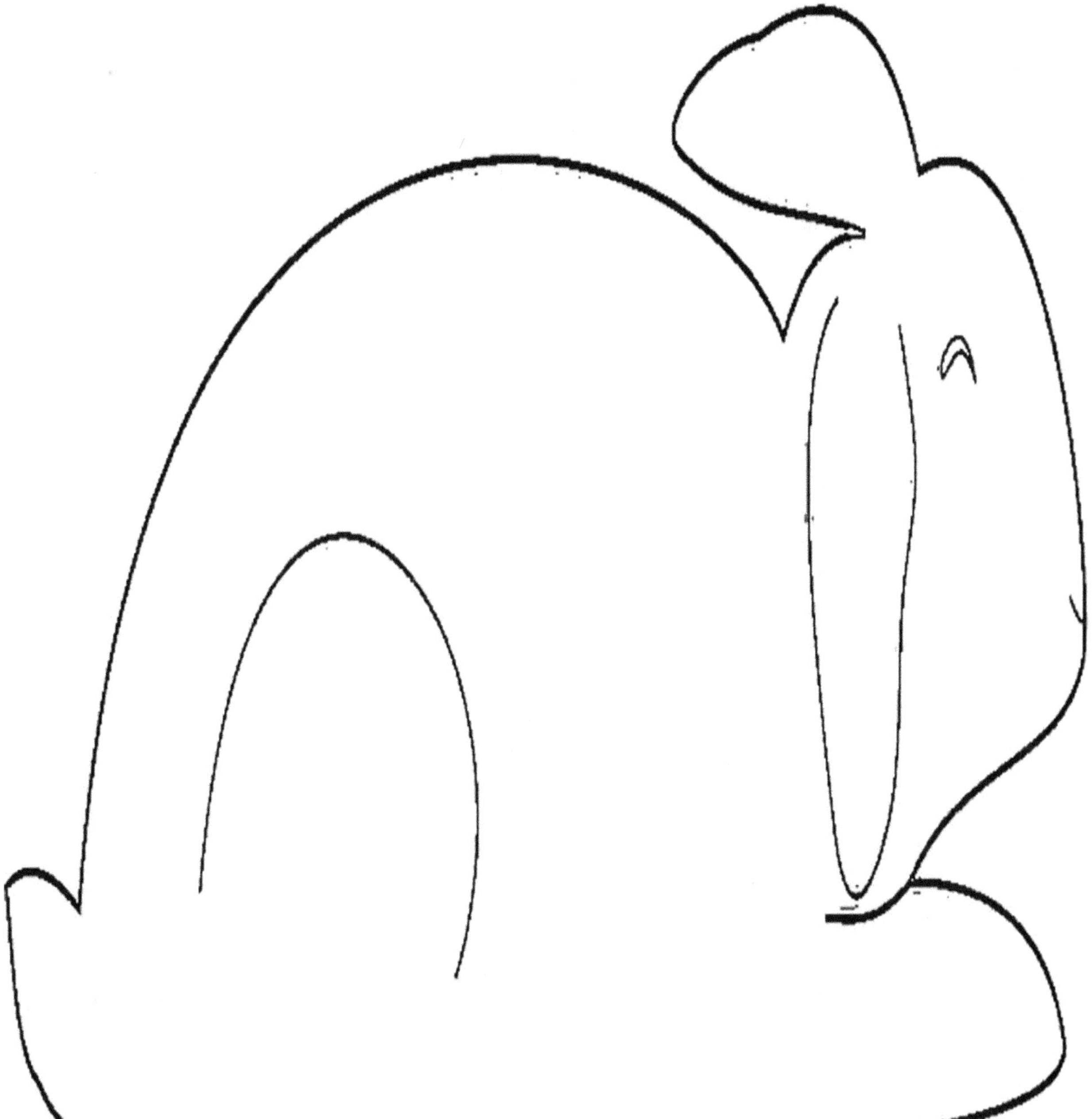

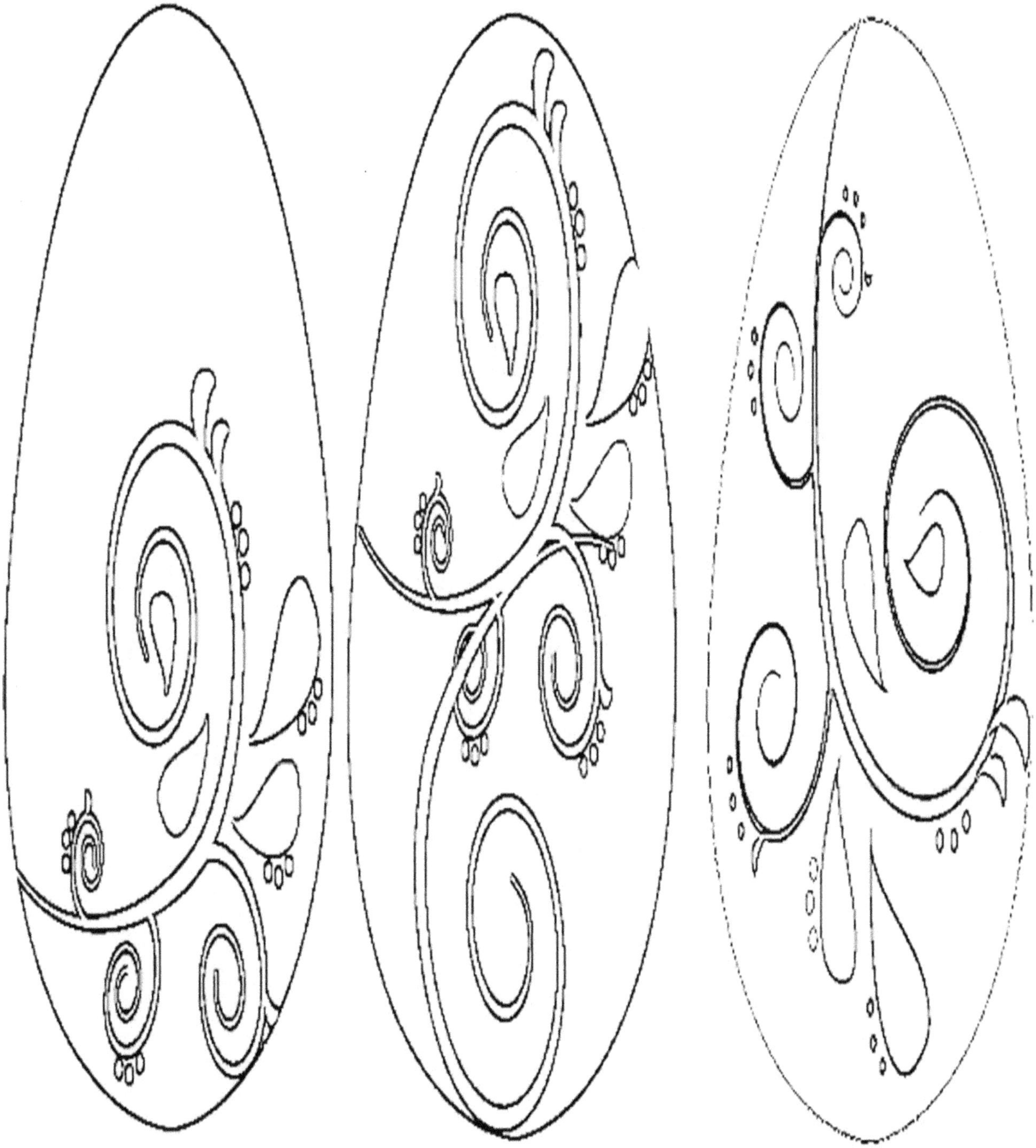

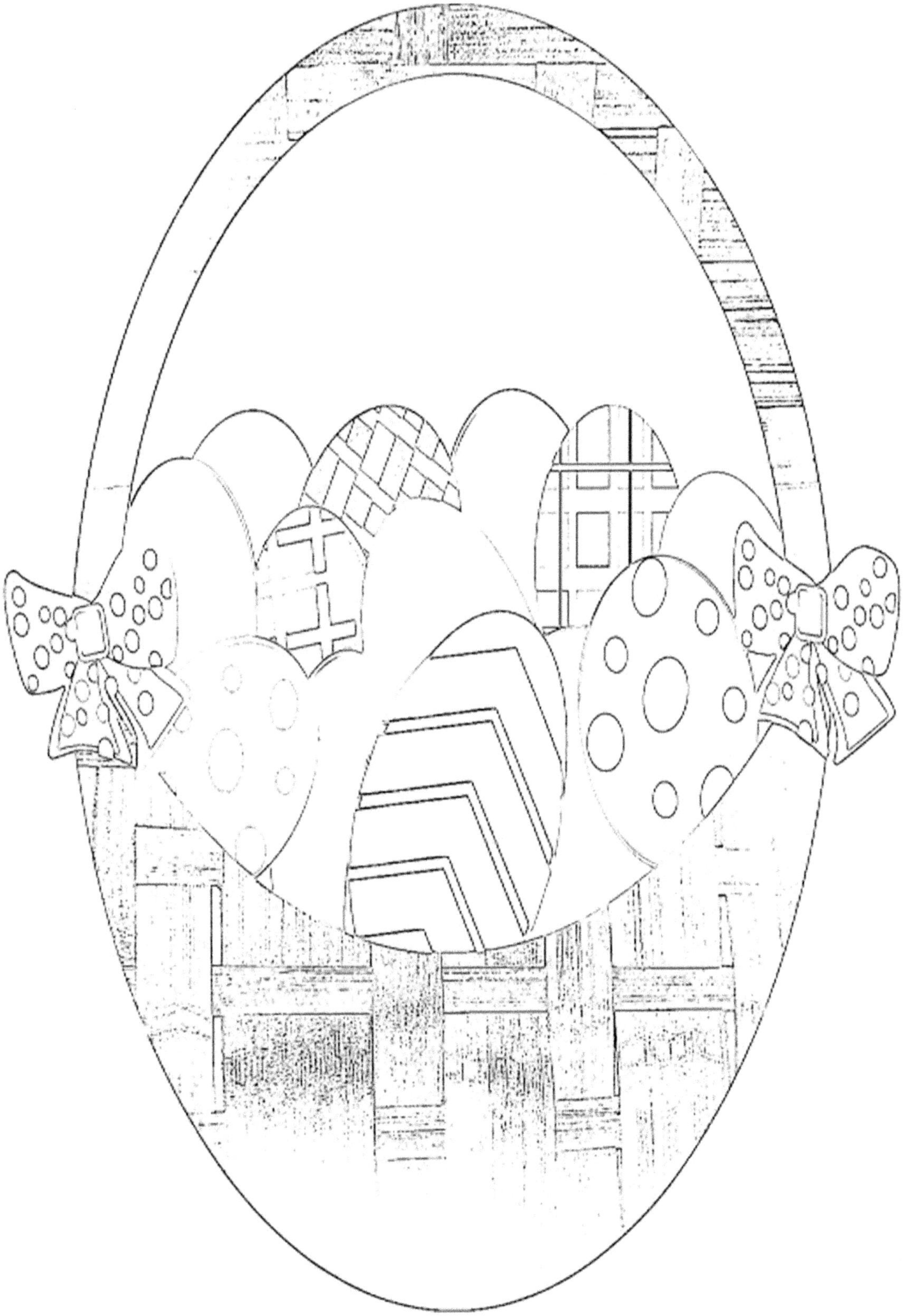

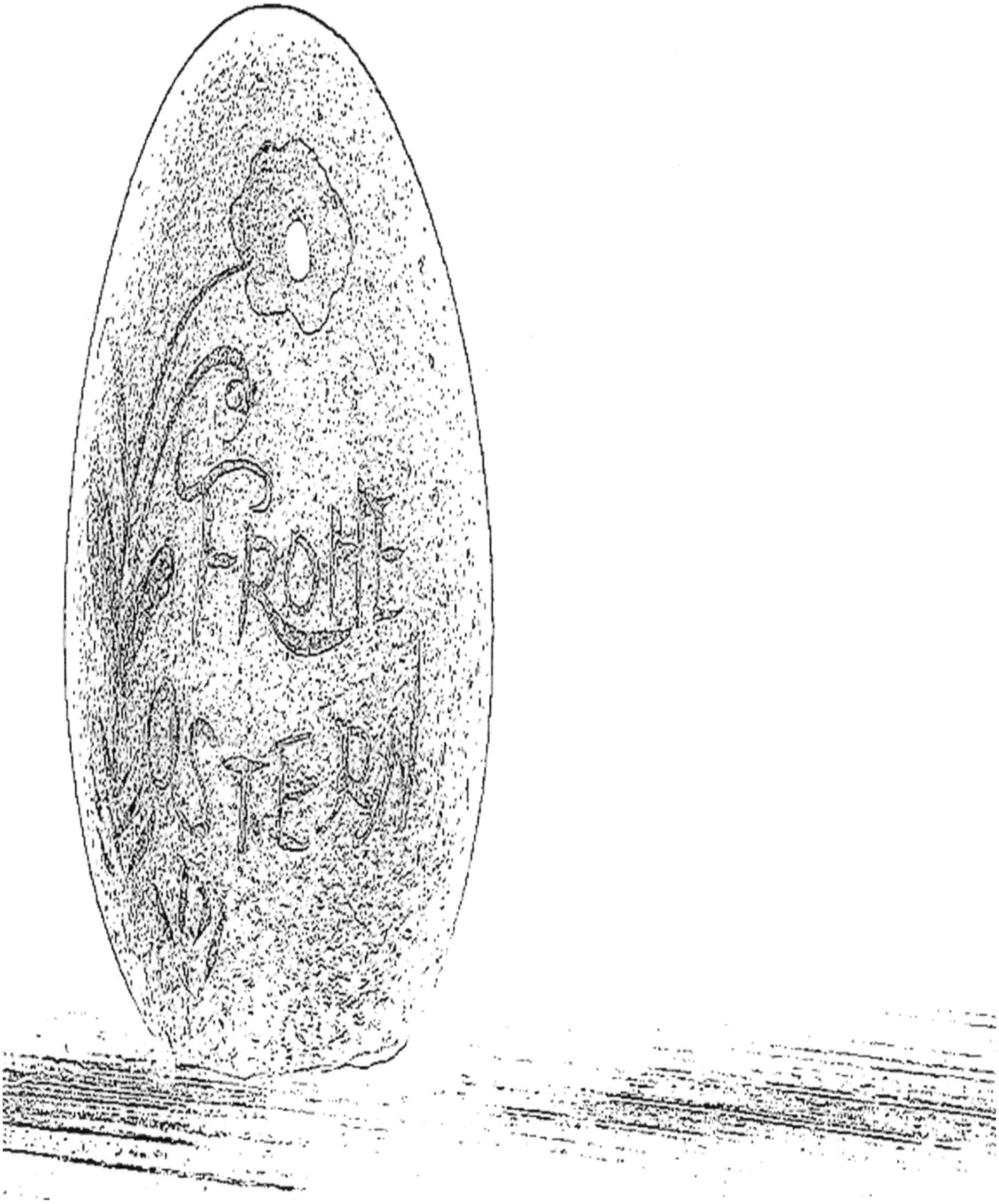

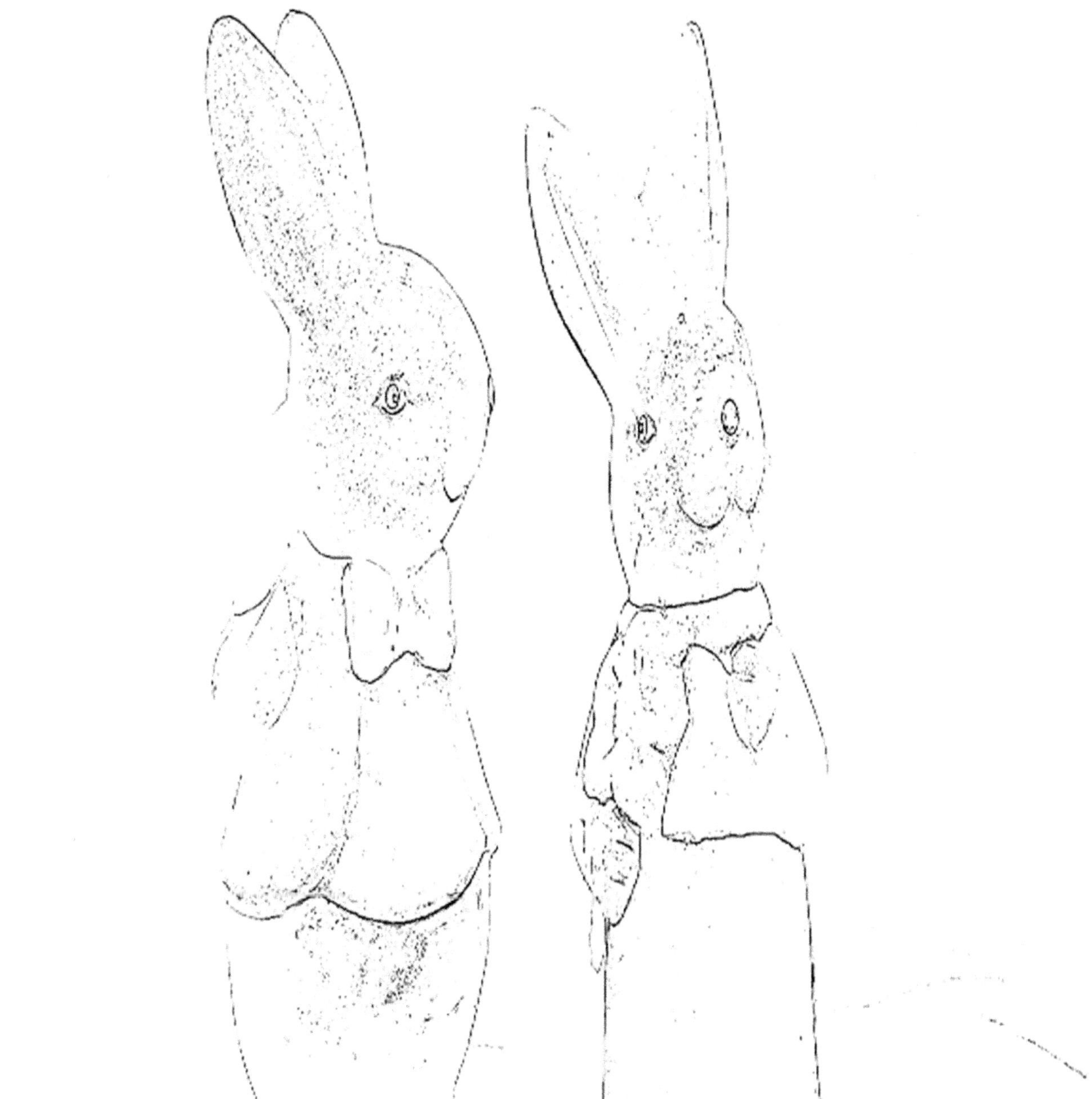

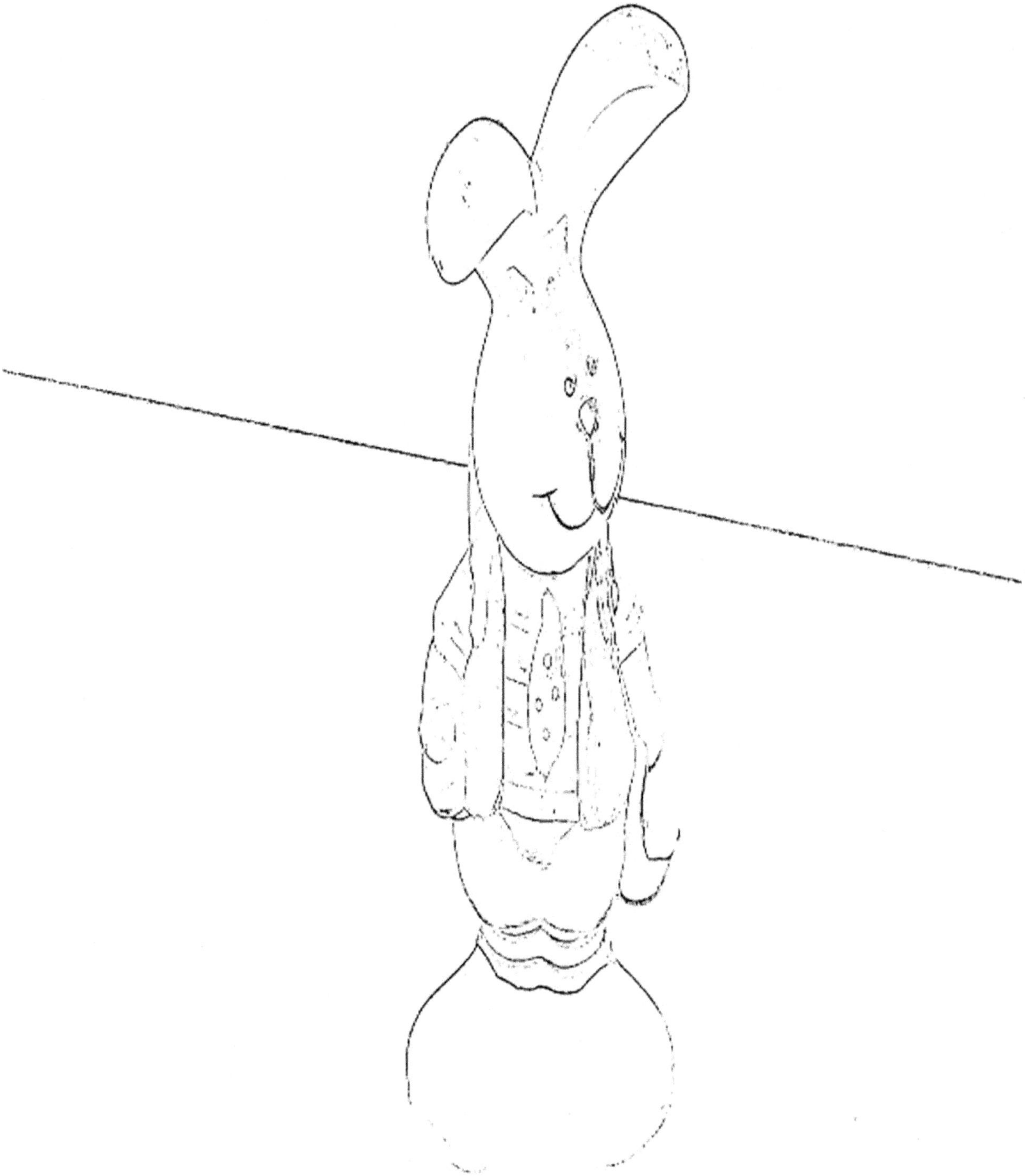

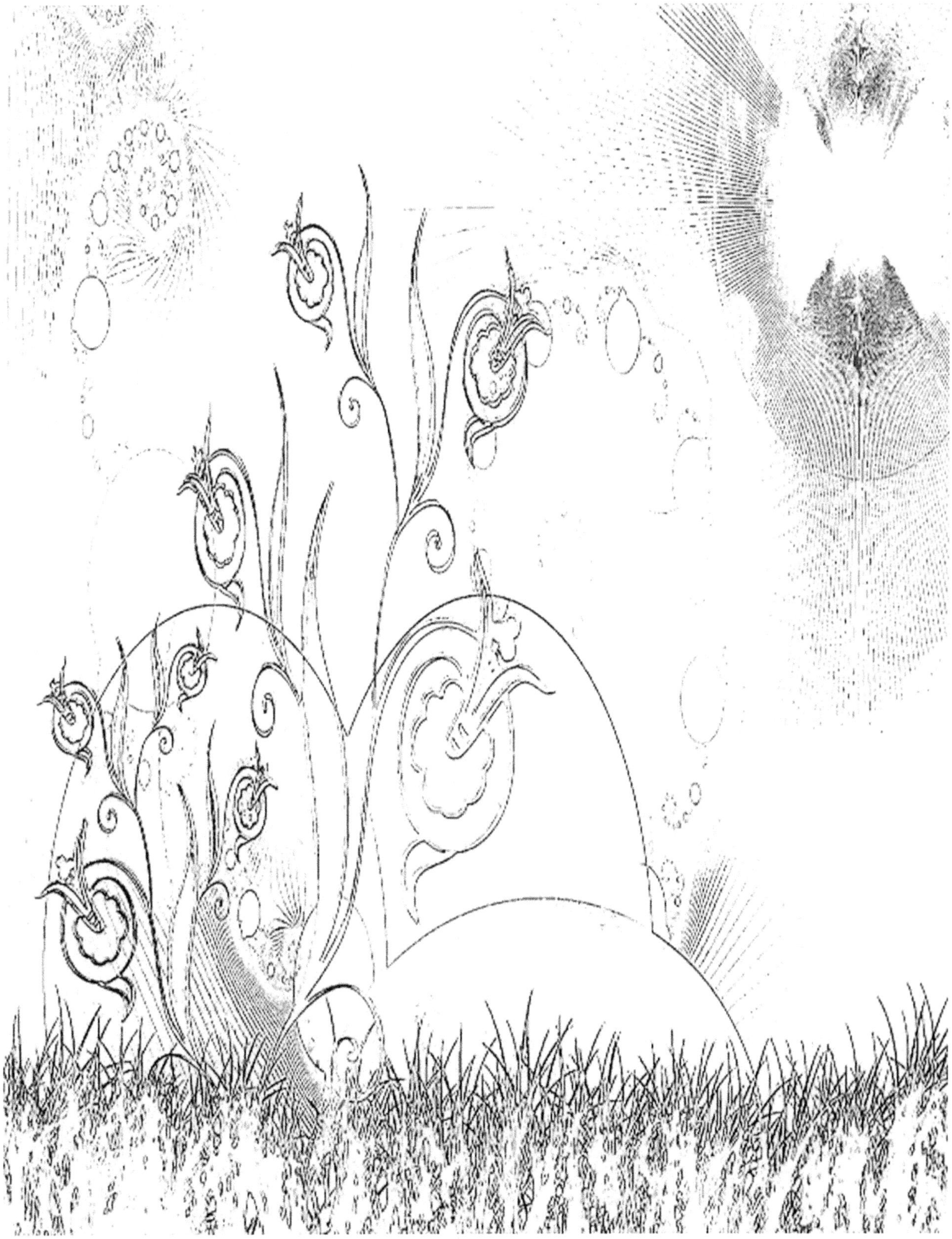

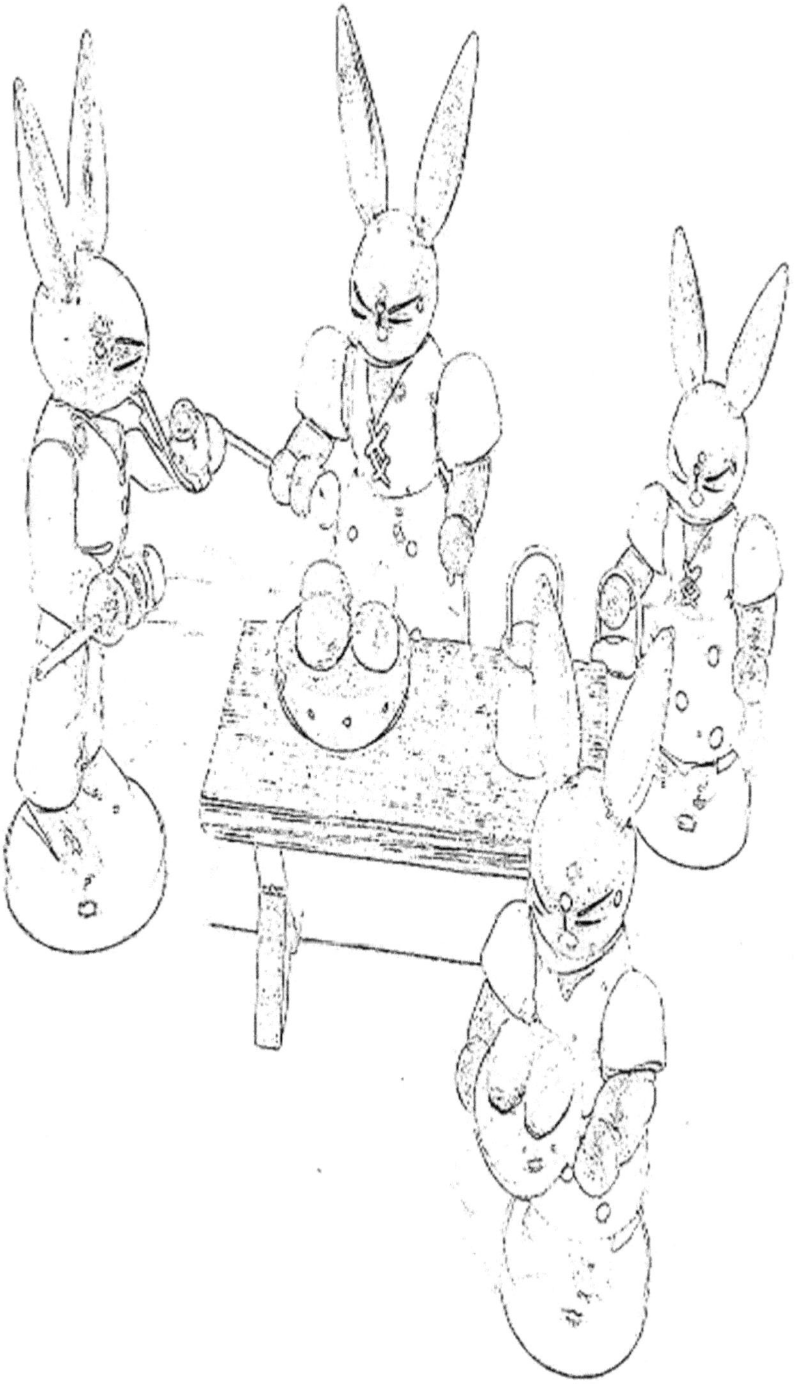

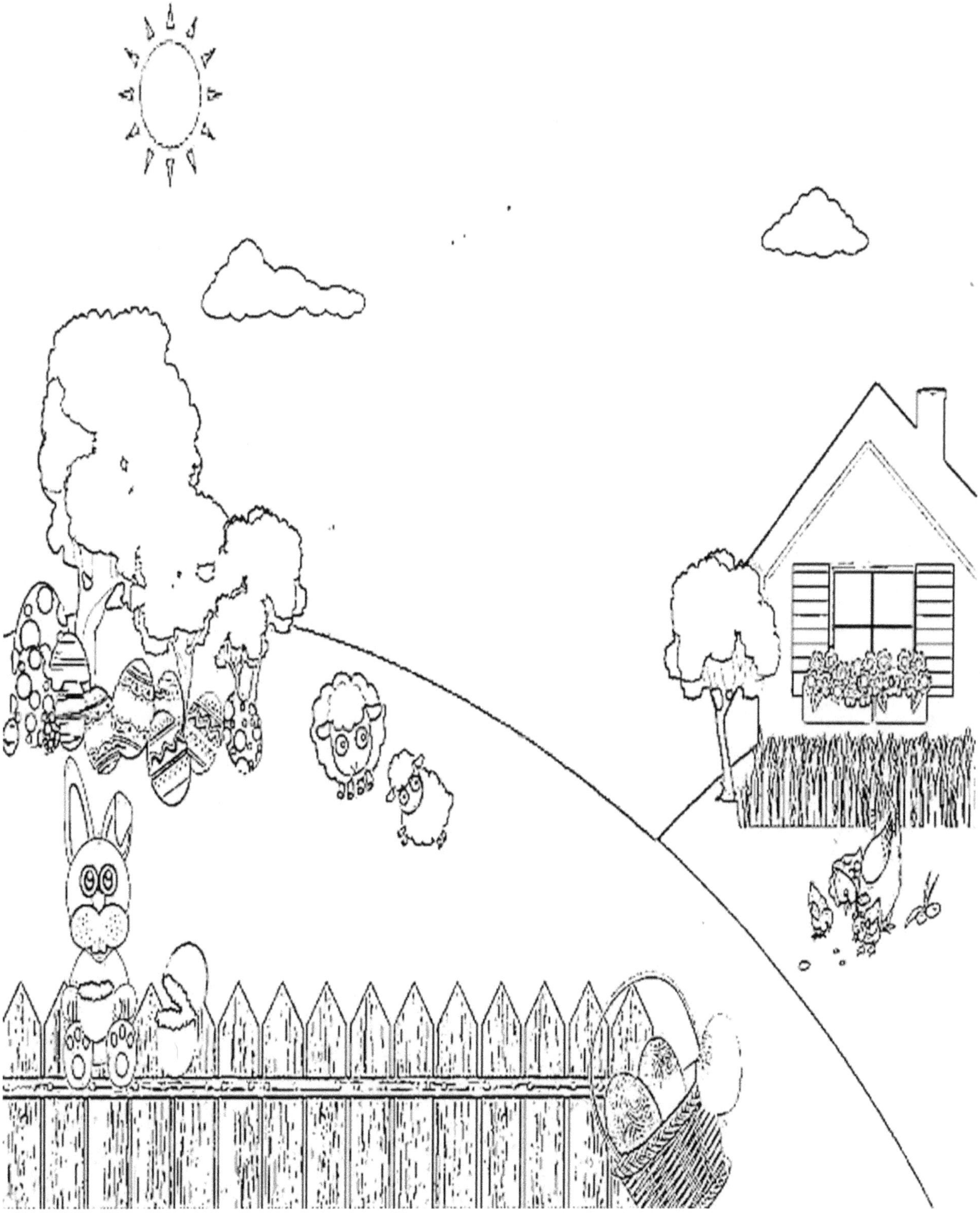

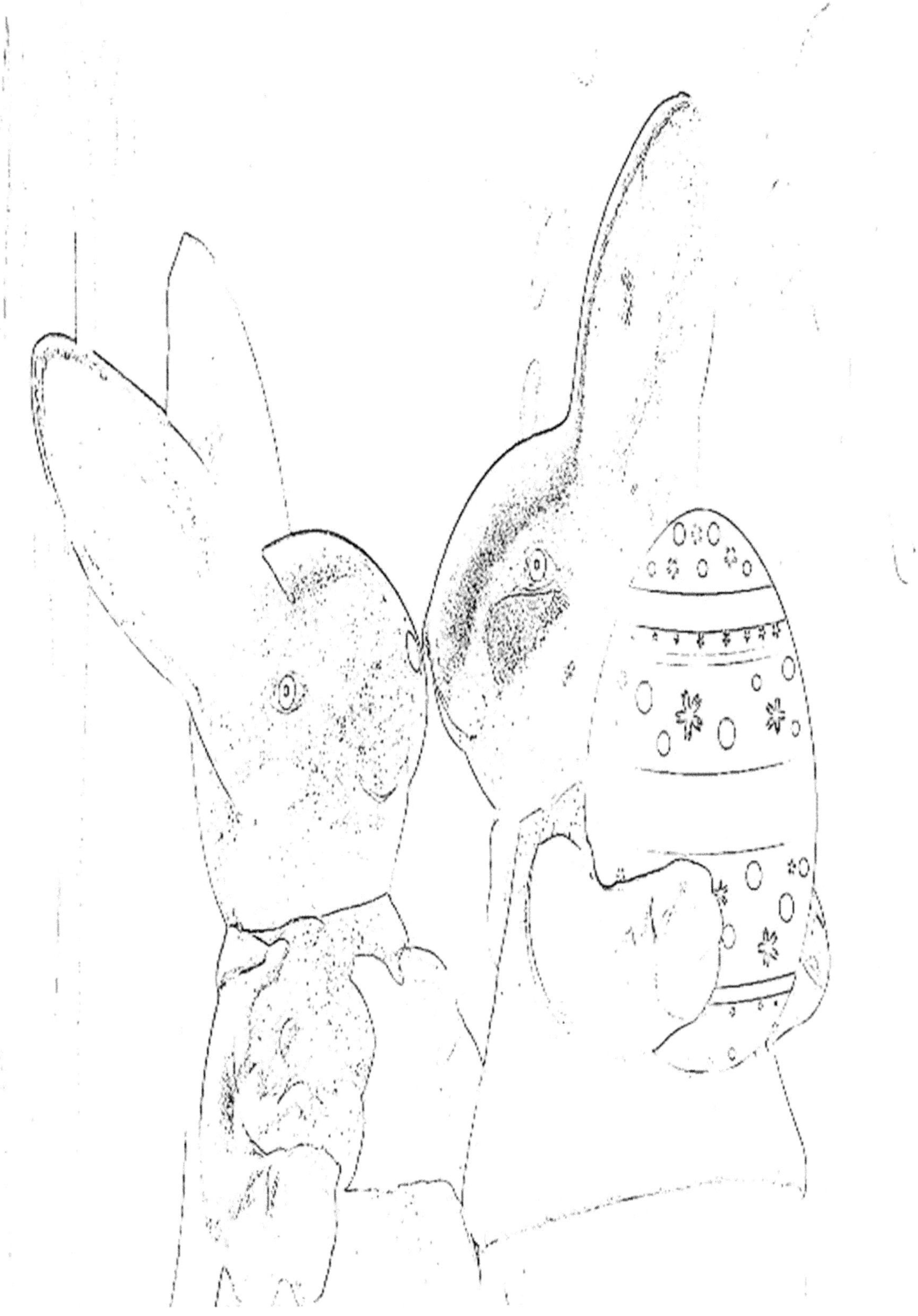

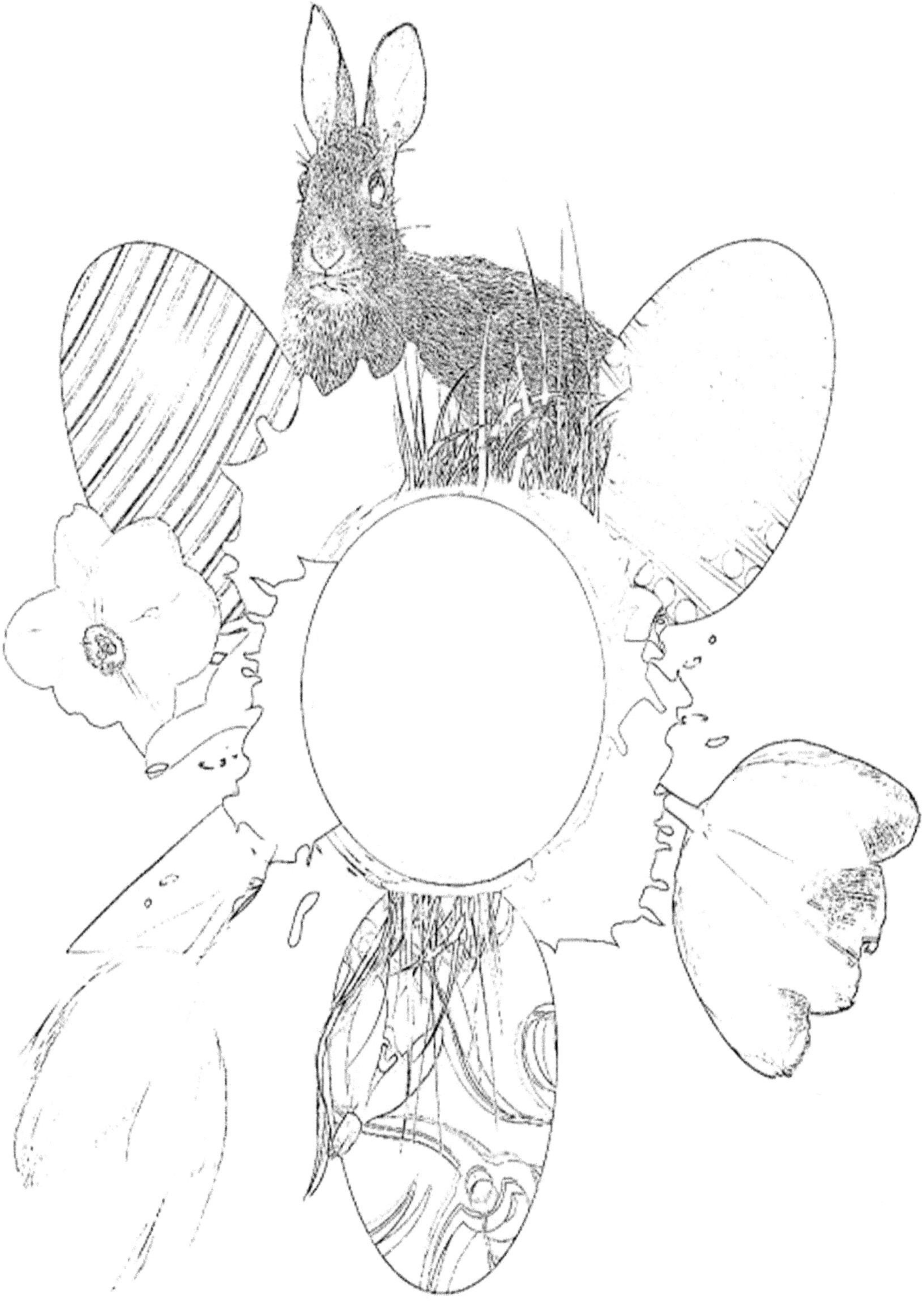

Note

www.ingramcontent.com/pod-product-compliance
Lightning Source LLC
Chambersburg PA
CBHW080632190526
45169CB00009B/3373
9781530508525